How to Write with Flair

Heather Holleman

Heather Holleman teaches composition classes at Penn State. Dr. Holleman earned the *Moscow Prize for Excellence in Teaching Composition* and *Rackham's Most Outstanding Graduate Student Instructor Award* while at the University of Michigan. She also served as a Sweetland Fellow in the University of Michigan Writing Center. At Penn State, Dr. Holleman directed the Excellence in Communication Certificate Program for the College of Liberal Arts while providing leadership and training for the Advanced Writing instructors.

ISBN 9781453721209

Lesson Two contains a list of analysis verbs reprinted with permission from the author, Jessica O'Hara. Lesson Three includes excerpts from food blogs published in the *New York Times* and are reprinted with permission from the authors, Mark Bittman and Sam Sifton. Examples of student writing are reprinted with permission.

To the students

Ready in Five. . .

Contents

Acknowledgments

I wish to thank my husband, Ashley, for supporting my teaching and writing all these years. I extend special recognition to my daughters, Sarah and Kate, who cheered me on when I talked about writing this book. I would also like to thank my graphic designer, Rachel Schrock, for her cover design. I am indebted to Jennifer Norton, Lauren Kooistra, and Andrea Babich for offering their typesetting and editorial expertise for this manuscript. Finally, to my amazing neighbors and friends who challenged me to publish this book and to *live* with flair, I am forever grateful.

Introduction: Even You!

My students recently confessed their addiction to the *Food Network*. They know more about roasting and stewing than I ever did as a college student. One day, I found myself explaining a writing technique by claiming, "Look, it's just like stirring the pot and then adding garnish." I connected my love of writing with their love of food, and soon, we had a common language.

By regularly comparing their writing tasks to the cooking feats they watch so religiously on television, I realized the comparison makes sense. In every class, I scurry about the classroom like an eager chef spouting off directions to my assistants (technically, my *Sous-Chefs*): Add some flavor with this delicious verb! Put in that secret ingredient of a semicolon or comma! Stir the pot and vary those sentence patterns! Don't forget to garnish! Don't forget to plate it with flair!

They try my recipe (just five steps), and suddenly they create masterpieces. I see it every semester. Writing with flair—like adding spices to a roast—results from following simple steps; once you get the basics down, you discover that great writing isn't reserved for the chosen few born with some gift. Anybody—even you—can write like a professional.

Anybody—even you—can write like a professional.

Like cooking, writing a paper with flair means you know how to fill a page with the right grammatical structures in the right amounts. But grammar is hard, and unless you had intensive grammar in elementary or middle school, you probably don't know what a subjunctive adjective is or a subordinating conjunction for that matter. You probably don't care about predicate nominatives or unclear antecedents (hardly anyone does, except maybe grammar teachers).

What you *do* care about is communicating well, with a unique voice, in memorable ways. You want to be a chef who creates a masterpiece of a meal without having to memorize a cookbook of rules.

The problem with grammar guides these days (like the other one you might have on your desk right now) is that they speak the foreign language of grammar rules. That's like asking the great chef Auguste Escoffier to teach us how to make a soufflé in French. Instead, we need a translator who can make the language understandable. What if you learned five steps instead? Well, in that case, you might actually write.

What if you learned five steps instead?

My friend brought me a special cookbook last month. It's a five-ingredient cookbook. Just five ingredients! I never cook elaborate recipes. I get overwhelmed, intimidated, and frustrated. But with just five ingredients to manage? Anyone can do that. So guess what? I'm cooking amazing recipes nearly every day. *How to Write with Flair* reminds me of that five-ingredient cookbook. Before you know it, you'll be writing fantastic things. Gone is the frustration. Gone is the intimidation. Overwhelmed? Never! Instead, you're having the time of your life. You're enjoying yourself because writing, when broken down into simple tips, becomes *fun*.

All great chefs enjoy the process: they lick spoons, sample sauces, inhale aromas, and then eagerly share samples with the crowd. Great chefs love their creations. Might working with words invite this same pleasure?

Imagine we are in my kitchen before a great stew pot. We have just five ingredients we can use in the right combinations — and in the right amounts — to create a masterpiece. Think of *Flair* as our guide. Don't worry about burning the sauce or setting the whole place on fire. Just worry about having fun, creating something original, and celebrating the process.

~Dr. H

How to use *Flair*:

How to Write with Flair takes you through five lessons that guarantee improvement in your writing skills. It's OK if you haven't had a grammar class before. It's also OK if you're a grammar expert. Everybody can benefit from a quick brush-up on how to transform any piece of writing into a masterpiece. Emails, memos, résumés, cover letters, essays, research papers, love letters, blog entries, text messages, thank-you notes, Facebook status updates, holiday letters, or your next big novel might suddenly transform into something clever, memorable, and full of *flair*.

Lesson One: *Finding Flavor*
Learn to eliminate feeble verbs and spice up the sentence with powerful, image-provoking verbs.

Lesson Two: *Secret Ingredients*
Employ the tricks that skilled writers juggle in their writing. Assure instant credibility and complexity to any paragraph by knowing how to masterfully use semicolons, dashes, parentheses, colons, and commas.

Bon Appétit!

Lesson One:
Finding Flavor

Lesson One: Finding Flavor

Welcome to the VERB!

Lesson One teaches us to find strong, flavorful verbs. **The verb invigorates your writing to transform a dull sentence into a vibrant one.** Once you complete Lesson One, you'll know how to add some flavor to every sentence. A verb (for those of us who haven't touched a grammar book in our lives) expresses something happening (action, occurrence, existence). This lesson teaches you to avoid verbs that don't SHOW anything happening.

> *Readers like to **see** what's going on in a sentence just like diners like to taste delectable flavors.*

First, we must memorize a little jingle.

I want you to sing the following list to the tune of "Jingle Bells" (or any song you can think of to help you remember).

BE – BEING – BEEN AM – IS – ARE WAS – WERE – HAS – HAVE – HAD DO – DOES – DID – CAN – and COULD SEEMS – APPEARS – EXISTS.	*These verbs represent bland actions and evoke no mental image. They often reflect states of being.*

The song cements the verbs in your mind. Now ELIMINATE these verbs from your writing. OK, maybe that's too harsh.

Instead, USE SPARINGLY (like maybe one or two in a paragraph). Think of these verbs as water, or worse, chicken broth. Chicken broth is fine; it's a good base to a recipe, but it *bores*. Nobody wants to eat an entire pot of chicken broth just like nobody wants to read a paper filled with bland verbs.

Now sing the song again. This time designate an image to go along with each verb. *Right.* It doesn't happen. These verbs represent *feeble* actions. In other words, these verbs inhibit strong images because they describe what is, what was, or what will be in a general, existential sort of way.

> I am.
> I was.
> We were.
> *Somebody please pass the salt!*

Whenever you write a sentence, stop, sing the song, and see if weak verbs clutter your writing. Then, go to your spice cabinet of strong verbs (see the list of my favorite ones on pages 24-27), and insert a few. You'll be amazed at how good your sentences sound.

Start practicing! Take a look at the revisions below:

I *am being* stubborn about not using weak verbs.
I **insist** on using strong verbs.

There are few weak verbs in the essay.
This essay **contains** few weak verbs.

I *appear to have* lost my glasses.
I **lost** my glasses.

When you write any sentence, see if you can take out the bland verb and add in some flavor. Notice the difference below:

Bland: This research opportunity **appears** that it will prepare me for future laboratory experience.

Revision: This research opportunity **will prepare** me for future laboratory experience.

Bland: My background in biology and genetics **is** what I feel will help me in the position.

Revision: My background in biology and genetics **helps** me in this position.

Can you see how a simple elimination of a weak verb spices up the sentence? But we still might do better here. *Do you see images in your mind as you read these sentences?* Might a more flavorful verb produce a more memorable sentence? I remember the taste of the chocolate cheesecake I ate last night. I can hardly remember the bread. Let's find a memorable, cheesecake type of verb.

Try this:

- This research opportunity will (**strengthen, hone**) my laboratory skills.

    I see someone working hard, like someone building muscles.

- My background in biology and genetics (**certifies, authorizes, qualifies**) me for this position.

    I see someone with a certificate or license to work.

Finding strong verbs to create a memorable image takes a little imagination. For example, if I asked you to describe what you see outside your window, you might write:

The leaves are on the ground.

You just served up pudding when you could have offered *crème brulee* (or, in the words of one student, you served Ramen noodles when you could have offered Pasta Alfredo).

Take out the weak verb (are), and add in a verb that shows something happening. Choose a verb that creates a mood regarding these leaves. You might go through the alphabet and think of at least 26 more vivid verbs.

Like this:

> The leaves (arrive, blanket, cavort, dance, explode, fan, grapple, hover, illustrate, jet-ski, kiss, lavish, mourn, nod, oscillate, pummel, query, ricochet, skip, tousle, usher, vacillate, wander, xanthiate, yearn, or zip) on the ground.

You *verbed* that sentence. You found some flavor and some *flair!* You added *ambiance* and *vibe.* "Blanket" creates a different mood from "bombard," so use verbs that create the type of feeling you hope to covey.

You try: Write a sentence with a vivid verb that creates an image.

1. I was at the party. _____

2. We seem to have joy._____

3. She was on the couch._____

4. The paper was hard for me to write._____

5. There appears to be a storm coming._____

Answer Key:
1. I (crashed, haunted, graced, popped in at) the party.
2. We (frolic, celebrate, whoop, relish, delight, enjoy).
3. She (lounges, spreads out, faints, sleeps, expires, melts) on the couch.
4. The paper (conquered, schooled, challenged, taxed) me.
5. A storm (brews, forms, builds).

Finally, remember that when you find the vivid verb, you need to **put the verb in its strongest form.** When you cook with various ingredients, you often chop off all the unnecessary parts that nobody wants to find floating around in the soup. Celery tops. Fish heads. Onion skin. Once you get rid of the "Jingle Bell" verbs, and replace them with some vivid ones, you still have to find the best, most concise form of that verb. It's like peeling the garlic clove to free it from its annoying, flaky skin. It's like chopping off the celery tops.

Intensify your flavor by chopping off the "ing," "ed," and the phrase "there is (are, were, seems)."

Imagine again that I ask you to describe your goals for the semester. You write:

- I **am excited** to be in this class. I **am planning** on improving my writing. **There is** a lot to learn. **There are** many ideas in this book.

Revise to:

- The class **excites** me. I **plan** to improve my writing. This class **offers** a lot to learn. This book **teaches** many ideas.

Eliminate feeble verbs, insert vivid ones, and intensify their flavor by using the present tense form. Whenever I revise any piece of writing, I start with the verbs. It takes practice, but soon, you'll find yourself naturally choosing creative verbs that produce powerful feelings in your readers.

1. Eliminate weak verbs.

2. Insert vivid verbs.

3. Put the verb in the strongest form, usually present tense (take off the "ed" or "ing").

Start with the verbs!

You try: Put these sentences in their strongest form. I've modeled some possibilities for the first three. You can try the next seven.

Bland: Spiced:

1. She is hoping to   *She **desires** a*
    become a writer.   *writing career.*

2. I was wondering   *I **wonder** what makes*
    what makes a good writer. *a good writer.*

3. I am being silly   *My nerves **embarrass***
    about being nervous.   *me.*

4. We already are liking this class.

5. It is not so difficult to be writing with flair.

6. She is using all sorts of weak verbs.

7. The verb list is needed to write my paper.

8. There are many rules of grammar I don't understand.

9. There is time for me to learn because of this handbook.

10. I am planning on becoming a doctor.

Some possible revisions:

4. We **like** this class already.
5. I **write easily** with flair.
6. She **uses** weak verbs.
7. I **need** the verb list.
8. Many rules of grammar **confuse** me.
9. This handbook **allows** time for me to learn.
10. I **plan to pursue** medicine.

Below (and on the next few pages), you'll find close to 500 verbs to use in any document (an essay, a blog entry, an email, a résumé, a Facebook status update, a love letter). Keep the verb list handy, and start experimenting with flavor! This particular list helps with papers that require **analysis** of a text. Instead of writing, "the author was saying," you can say, "the author debunks (elaborates, illuminates, or even rationalizes)."

Abates	Arranges	Clarifies	Conveys	Diminishes
Abdicates	Articulates	Clutters	Convinces	Disables
Abolishes	Assimilates	Colors	Copies	Disabuses
Accelerates	Associates	Collapses	Correlates	Discerns
Accentuates	Asserts	Collides	Corresponds	Discovers
Acclimates	Assists	Compels	Counsels	Discredits
Accommodates	Associates	Compiles	Creates	Discusses
Accomplishes	Assumes	Compliments	Credits	Disenfranchises
Acknowledges	Assures	Conceals	Criticizes	Disillusions
Acts	Authenticates	Concentrates	Critiques	Dismantles
Adapts	Awakens	Concludes	Debates	Dismisses
Addresses	Balances	Concocts	Debunks	Dispels
Adds	Becomes	Concurs	Decides	Displays
Adheres	Believes	Conceptualizes	Defies	Disproves
Advances	Betrays	Combines	Defines	Dissects
Advises	Blends	Compiles	Delineates	Dissents
Advocates	Boasts	Commences	Delivers	Dissolves
Affects	Bolsters	Communicates	Deludes	Distinguishes
Affirms	Brags	Compares	Demands	Distributes
Alerts	Bridges	Configures	Demolishes	Documents
Alleviates	Brings forth	Confirms	Demonstrates	Dominates
Allows	Builds	Confronts	Denotes	Draws
Alludes	Calculates	Connects	Depends	Dramatizes
Amazes	Cajoles	Conserves	Depicts	Educates
Amplifies	Camouflages	Consolidates	Depletes	Elaborates
Analyzes	Captures	Constitutes	Derives	Elevates
Antagonizes	Catalogues	Constructs	Describes	Elucidates
Anticipates	Cements	Consumes	Designates	Eludes
Applies	Champions	Contradicts	Detains	Embarks
Appraises	Changes	Contemplates	Determines	Embellishes
Appropriates	Characterizes	Contests	Develops	Embodies
Arbitrates	Chronicles	Contrasts	Diagnoses	Emboldens
Architects	Circumvents	Controls	Dictates	Emphasizes
Argues	Claims	Construes	Differentiates	Empties
Arouses	Classifies	Converts	Dismisses	Emulates

Enables	Forces	Intends	Mimics	Portrays
Encourages	Forecasts	Instigates	Mirrors	Possesses
Enflames	Foreshadows	Integrates	Mobilizes	Precedes
Engineers	Forges	Interprets	Mocks	Precludes
Enhances	Fosters	Invents	Models	Predisposes
Enlightens	Frames	Investigates	Modifies	Prefaces
Enriches	Fulfills	Invigorates	Molds	Presents
Ensnares	Furthers	Invites	Monitors	Prioritizes
Entails	Gambles	Invokes	Monopolizes	Probes
Entitles	Generates	Involves	Motivates	Produces
Epitomizes	Gestures	Isolates	Multiplies	Prohibits
Equates	Glorifies	Jettisons	Navigates	Projects
Eradicates	Grapples	Joins	Negates	Prolongs
Establishes	Gratifies	Judges	Neglects	Promotes
Evaluates	Guides	Justifies	Negotiates	Propels
Evolves	Harass	Kamikazes	Normalizes	Proposes
Evokes	Harmonizes	Lacks	Nurtures	Protests
Exacerbates	Hides	Lavishes	Observes	Protracts
Examines	Highlights	Launches	Obscures	Proves
Exaggerates	Hinges	Lectures	Opens	Provides
Excavates	Hypothesize	Legitimizes	Optimizes	Provokes
Exemplifies	Identifies	Leverages	Orchestrates	Punctuates
Exhibits	Ignores	Links	Ordains	Pursues
Exonerates	Illegitimates	Lists	Orders	Queries
Expands	Illuminates	Locates	Orients	Questions
Expends	Illustrates	Maintains	Organizes	Qualifies
Experiments	Imagines	Magnifies	Outlines	Ranks
Explains	Impels	Makes	Overlooks	Ratifies
Exploits	Implements	Mandates	Paints	Rationalizes
Explores	Implies	Maneuvers	Parallels	Recalls
Exposes	Improves	Mangles	Paralyzes	Recoils
Expresses	Includes	Manifests	Penetrates	Recognizes
Expunges	Incorporates	Manipulates	Perfects	Recommends
Extends	Indicates	Marshals	Performs	Refers
Extricates	Infers	Masters	Personifies	Reflects
Fabricates	Inflicts	Materializes	Persuades	Refutes
Facilitates	Informs	Measures	Pinpoints	Reinforces
Familiarizes	Initiates	Mediates	Pioneers	Reinstates
Fashions	Inquires	Mends	Places	Reiterates
Fine-tunes	Insinuates	Mentions	Points out	Rejects
Fixates	Insists	Merits	Ponders	Relates
Focuses	Inspects	Meshes	Polarizes	Relies

Relinquishes
Remedies
Reminds
Reminisces
Renews
Renounces
Requires
Represents
Resembles
Resources
Restores
Reveals
Reviews
Revises
Ridicules
Ruins
Scrutinizes
Seduces
Seems
Segues
Sells
Sensationalizes
Separates
Shadows
Sharpens
Shapes
Sheds
Sheds light on
Showcases
Shows
Sifts
Signifies
Simplifies
Simulates
Specifies
Speculates
Spins
Spotlights
Spurs
Standardizes
States
Stems
Translates
Transcribes

Uncovers
Underlies
Underlines
Undermines
Unearths
Unfurls
Unmasks
Unveils
Urges
Uses
Utilizes
Validates
Verifies
Vilifies
Visits
Visualizes
Vitalizes
Volunteers
Weakens
Weighs
Widens
Wins
Withdraws
Witnesses
Writes
Yields
X-rays
Zaps
Zeros -in

Aroma: Mood and Connotation

You can create a mood by the verb you choose. As you analyze a text, for example, you might say the author "sheds light on" or "sharpens" our understanding of the topic. These verbs create a very different mood from "the author sensationalizes" or "the author scrutinizes" the topic.

In materials you write that shape an identity for yourself (résumé, cover letter, or mission statement), you want to choose verbs carefully. Pick verbs with positive connotations.

Make a note of positive (+) or negative (-) connotations certain verbs evoke. If the connotation is neutral, put a circle (o).

Add Your Own:

1. _____
2. _____
3. _____
4. _____
5. _____
6. _____
7. _____
8. _____
9. _____
10. _____

For those of us writing résumés and cover letters, compiling categories of verbs allows for quick reference. Since most of us will develop professional materials at some point in our lives, I include a list of verbs grouped together to reflect types of skills.

Circle the ones you like, and practice using them in your own résumés and cover letters. These use the "ed" because you'll be describing actions in the past. Drop the "ed" if you currently hold a position where you utilize these skills.

Leadership or Management Verbs:

achieved, administered, arranged, articulated, assigned, attained, authored, chaired, competed, conceived, conducted, contracted, convened, coordinated, created, delegated, designed, developed, directed, earned, effected, employed, executed, facilitated, influenced, initiated, instituted, instructed, intervened, invented, investigated, managed, mastered, modeled, organized, oversaw, planned, presented, presided, protected, recommended, regulated, represented, resolved, shaped, solved, specified, succeeded, supervised, visualized

Teamwork Verbs:

articulated, arranged, briefed, clarified, collaborated, communicated, competed, confronted, contacted, convened, coordinated, delegated, elicited, employed, encouraged, endured, enlisted, exchanged, explained, facilitated, fostered, influenced, initiated, inquired, instructed, interpreted, intervened, interviewed, introduced, listened, mediated, motivated, negotiated, participated, represented, resolved, responded, shaped, shared, solicited, supported

Technical Skills Verbs:

analyzed, applied, assessed, calculated, catalogued,
categorized, channeled, coded, compiled, computed,
conducted, defined, delivered, derived, designed, developed,
devised, drafted, formulated, implemented, inspected,
installed, mastered, monitored, operated, processed,
programmed, protected, provided, published, recorded,
regulated, repaired, reported, reproduced, responded,
searched, shared, simulated, solved, supported, systematized,
tested, trained, translated, tutored, updated, wrote

~~~~

This concludes Lesson One. Hopefully, you'll never think of
verbs the same way again. When you pick your verb, think of
spices. Think of ginger, rosemary, cumin, or pepper.

Verbs add *flavor.*

Remember to keep an ongoing list of new verbs. I just heard a
student say he "fiddled" with his paragraph, and another
student claimed she needed to "fritter away" some excess
wording. I'm adding those to my own spice cabinet of great
verbs.

Lesson Two:
Secret Ingredients

Lesson Two: Secret Ingredients

Welcome to Cool Punctuation Marks!

$$; - - ( ) : ,$$

Semicolon, dashes, parentheses, colon, comma

Now that you know how to find a strong verb for every sentence, let's try to add flair to *entire paragraphs*. Lesson Two teaches us to use advanced grammar (semicolons, dashes, parentheses, colons, and commas) to create varied sentence patterns. And when you stir up your sentences, you create complexity, a written voice, and (of course) coolness.

I read a lot; magazines, novels, the newspaper, blogs, textbooks, and academic journals pass over my desk or computer screen every day. Years ago, I began to notice a pattern in the types of writing that seem to get published. I noticed that good writing followed a recipe of sorts — as if the writers knew some secret code — that made it memorable. In fact, I began to observe the pattern in so many published articles and essays, I had to codify it. And now, I present it to you:

Great writers use cool punctuation in every paragraph. They juggle the Big 5: semicolons, dashes, parentheses, colons, and commas.

It's refreshing how simple it is! Last night I picked up a new bestselling novel at the library. Sure enough, the first paragraph painted a world with strong verbs, and, you guessed it: a semicolon here, a colon there, some dashes sprinkled next, and then some parentheses all housed within perfectly placed commas.

Try it! Start carefully reading published pieces of writing and locate the five secret ingredients. At this very moment, I'm reading the Food and Wine section of the *New York Times*. I think the food critics for the *New York Times* might have the best jobs around (besides teaching writing). These folks get to eat and then write about it—my two favorite things in the world—and get paid the big bucks to do it. Let's see what sort of secret ingredients writers in the food world use to enhance flavor.

As you read the examples in Lesson Two, try to remember these little code words. I'll explain them more in detail over the next few pages.

;	semicolon	= a romance
:	colon	= a teacher
—	dashes	= a shout
( )	parentheses	= a whisper
,	comma	= a key

Appearing below is one of the first food reviews I read today. Mark Bittman, the *New York Times* bestselling author of <u>Food Matters: A Guide to Conscious Eating with More Than 75 Recipes</u>, happens to describe a recipe for citrus salad. I love citrus, so I decide to read Bittman's piece. In his *New York Times* bestseller voice, he writes:

> The idea is a combination of grapefruit (I like pink), oranges (navels, though common, are terrific) and tangerines or clementines: any citrus fruit that's more sweet than sour. Peel the fruit: the easiest way is to cut off both ends at the poles so you have a flat surface to stand it upright, then cut as close to the pulp as possible, slicing off the skin in strips and removing as much bitter pith as possible. Slice the fruit into disks, then arrange it to show off the various colors and sizes. Sprinkle with salt — very important — and chopped or very thinly sliced red onion or shallot. The dressing is a mixture of sharp and sweet, designed to bring out the same contrasting flavors in the fruit: olive oil, sherry vinegar, a few drops of honey and a bit more citrus. I like a squeeze of lime, but lemon is also fine; a pinch of cayenne or a sprinkling of black pepper is all right but not essential.

> ~from Mark Bittman's "Allowing Citrus to Add Sunshine." *New York Times*, January 15, 2010.

This simple paragraph, if written without the secret ingredients, might have been exceedingly bland. After all, it's a *citrus salad* recipe. But Bittman knows the tricks: find some flavor with a few strong verbs (peel, cut, slice, sprinkle, designed), use some secret ingredients like the single semi-colon, well-placed parentheses, some proper commas, and the necessary colons. Notice, too, the dashes.

Underline or highlight the Big 5.

A Kitchen Experiment:

Let's remove the flair and see what that tastes like.

Read it aloud:

The idea is a combination of grapefruit. I like pink. You are going to use oranges. They are common but are terrific. Also use tangerines or clementines. You can use any citrus fruit that is more sweet than sour. You are peeling the fruit. The easiest way is to cut off both ends at the poles so you have a flat surface to stand it upright. Then you are cutting as close to the pulp as possible. You will slice the skin in strips. You will remove as much bitter pith as possible. You will be slicing the fruit into disks. Then you will be arranging it to show off the various colors and sizes. You will sprinkle with salt. This is important. You will also use very thinly sliced red onion or shallot. The dressing is a mixture of sharp and sweet. This is designed to bring out the same contrasting flavors in the fruit. The contrasting flavors are olive oil, sherry vinegar, a few drops of honey and a bit more citrus. I like a squeeze of lime. Lemon is also fine. I also like a pinch of cayenne or a sprinkling of black pepper. This is alright but not essential.

First of all, notice the absence of Lesson One vivid verbs. Second, observe the lack of Lesson Two secret ingredients.

What's different?

Let's look at the published paragraph again (with the flair highlighted).

The idea is a combination of grapefruit **(I like pink),** oranges **(navels, though common, are terrific)** and tangerines or **clementines: any** citrus fruit that's more sweet than sour. Peel the **fruit: the** easiest way is to cut off both ends at the poles so you have a flat surface to stand it **upright, then** cut as close to the pulp as possible, slicing off the skin in strips and removing as much bitter pith as possible. Slice the fruit into **disks, then** arrange it to show off the various colors and sizes. Sprinkle with salt—**very important**—and chopped or very thinly sliced red onion or shallot. The dressing is a mixture of sharp and **sweet, designed** to bring out the same contrasting flavors in the **fruit: olive** oil, sherry vinegar, a few drops of honey and a bit more citrus. I like a squeeze of lime, but lemon is also **fine; a pinch** of cayenne or a sprinkling of black pepper is all right but not essential.

Look at the visual flair!

Parentheses, colon, commas, dashes, semicolons all blend to create a reading experience. Just like a chef builds his recipe, use the Big 5 to build a paragraph.

Not every paragraph always needs to use these secret ingredients (that would overload the senses), but throughout a writing assignment, challenge yourself to sprinkle in these visual spices.

Let's look at one more Bittman review to notice the Big 5 in action. Recently, he reviewed a fried rice dish that sounded delicious. He writes:

> Like all fried-rice dishes, you must start this one with leftover rice; fresh rice is simply too moist. (Jean-Georges specifies jasmine rice, but white from Chinese takeout works nearly as well and is more convenient.) Unlike most, his is cooked in rendered chicken fat, which has incomparable flavor. With the chef's blessing, I tested the recipe with peanut oil, which is fine. Perhaps not surprisingly—this is a chef's recipe, after all—the process requires separate cooking processes: ginger and garlic are crisped, leeks softened, rice and eggs fried. But no step takes more than a couple of minutes, and the recipe is absolutely worth the effort.
>
> ~from Mark Bittman's "Fried Rice, Dressed Simply."
> *New York Times*, January 22, 2010

Check out the strong verbs (specifies, tested, requires, crisped, softened) and the Big 5.

Once again, imagine a bland version of the review:

> All fried rice dishes have leftover rice. Fresh rice is simply too moist. Jean-Georges has said to use jasmine rice. White rice from Chinese takeout works as well. This is more convenient. His is cooked in rendered chicken fat. This has incomparable flavor. The recipe was tested with peanut oil. I had the chef's blessing. I was not surprised about the separate cooking processes because it was a chef's recipe. The ginger and garlic were crisped. The leaks were softened. The rice and eggs were fried. This took no more than a couple of minutes. It is worth the effort.

Boring? Unfortunately.

Let's look at another example.

Yesterday, I read a review of a food dish I hadn't heard of before by the world-famous *New York Times* food critic, Sam Sifton. He writes:

> [The Hiramasa] was not a good dish. Nor was an octopus carpaccio with sun-dried tomatoes and fine herbs that, to the good, looked like a Chuck Close painting (to the bad, it tasted like one.) Baccalà was served three ways: as carpaccio, whipped, and baked. The carpaccio version, translucent and interesting, almost worked. The whipped one, though, loaded into a tube and pushed onto the plate in the manner of a cannoli filling, did not: too dense, too acidic. The baked — served with olives in a tomato sauce — was merely bland. And halibut confit in olive oil with chickpeas and a clam ragù made a mockery of the confit process; it was just halibut poached in olive oil, chewy and flavorless.

> ~ from Sam Sifton's "SD26." *New York Times*, December 2, 2009

Sifton narrates a past dining experience, so the verbs work best in the past, but notice their strength (whipped, tasted, loaded, pushed, served). He also includes *all* of the secret ingredients, in just the right places, to create good sentence rhythm.

Sifton and Bittman — whether they acknowledge it or not — seem to follow a pattern, don't they?

What if I told you that most great writers use this pattern? What if I told you that the secret ingredients grant instant complexity, cleverness, and credibility to your writing? Well, guess what? They do. In the next few pages, I'll tell you how to use the secret ingredients in understandable ways. So the next time you write anything, you can apply Lesson One and Lesson Two to create flair. Let's get started with the semicolon.

SEMICOLON

A semi-colon resembles a nail with a hook; that's what it looks like to me. So when I want to attach two sentences together, I need a nail and a hook. Simple. I tried for months to think of a cooking analogy that explains what a semi-colon does, and the best I conjured was this:

a toothpick.

You jam a toothpick down into two things you want to connect together (like bread to the sandwich meat).

A semi-colon, like a toothpick, is a way of holding two sentences together. But why would you want to attach two sentences together? Well, it's because the **two sentences belong to one another and enhance one another** just like two separate food items designed to bring out the flavor of the other. You combine a little lemon with your caviar. You serve the lamb with the mint jelly. You add the dill to your salmon. When you use a semi-colon, you tell the reader: try these together; it's delicious.

You tell the reader the ideas belong together in such an intimate way that they must *attach*.

A period, on the other hand, completes an idea and moves onto the next. A semi-colon lets one thought linger and blend into the other.

It's also like a *romance*. The sentences can't resist each other. They belong together, and the second sentence gazes back on the first; it wants you to adore that first sentence and learn more about it.

Turn back and take a look at how Bittman and Sifton use their semicolons. See how the ideas mingle? See how the second sentence really belongs with the first? Usually, the second sentence, like the mint jelly on lamb, *amplifies* the meaning in the first sentence.

- Writing this essay invigorates me; now that I have the secret ingredients, I astonish my readers.

   The second sentence explains more – amplifies – what you mean by the first.

- I hope to dominate these papers; I plan to use every bit of flair available.

   Sentence two explains what you will do to accomplish sentence one.

Instructions: Tell us whether each pairing of sentences would most benefit from a period or a semicolon. If you choose a semicolon, tell us why.

1. I plan on working for a restaurant. My degree enables me to be a chef or a manager.

2. My résumé sounds completely bland. I want my written voice to sound unique.

3. Reading this handbook makes me hungry. Right now I'd like to have a steak.

4. I never realized how many weak verbs I use. Every paper I have written before this class used some variation of "to be."

5. When you enjoy cooking, you look forward to consuming your creation. Does writing a paper nourish in the same way?

6. The semicolon creates credibility. Not many writers know how to use one properly.

7. Some people use semicolons like salt. That's fine, but too much salt, like too much cologne, can ruin the whole effect.

8. If I could learn to put a semicolon in every paragraph, I'd feel so clever. I just have to make sure I'm connecting two sentences that need to intimately attach.

9. A semicolon can also connect a series of phrases in the same way you might use a comma. That's a much easier rule to understand.

10. Let's move on to another secret ingredient. I'm getting tired of semicolon exercises.

NOTE: When you combine two sentences using a semicolon, you DO NOT capitalize the next sentence. That second sentence now flows with the first and does not require capitalization. You are not beginning a new sentence.

Answer Key:

1. Semicolon. The second sentence explains the reasoning for the first one.

2. Period. The second sentence begins a new idea separate from the first.

3. Semicolon. The second sentence clarifies or gives an example of the first.

4. Period. The second sentence begins a new idea separate from the first.

5. Period. The second sentence begins a new idea separate from the first.

6. Semicolon. The second sentence explains why the first sentence is true.

7. Period. The second sentence begins a new idea separate from the first.

8. Period. The second sentence begins a new idea separate from the first.

9. Period. The second sentence begins a new idea separate from the first.

10. Semicolon. The second sentence offers some explanation of the first.

DASHES

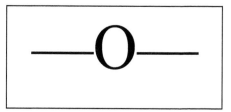

The dash shouts. And, by the way, think of the dash as "the dashes" because you ALWAYS NEED TWO (and on your keyboard, you must actually type two lines - - to make the dash. Most computers automatically elongate those two lines into one long dash — like that).

The dash shouts. It's the cayenne pepper of writing. It's the exclamation point within a sentence that makes everybody pause and listen. It stops the reader and makes him see something important — something he might otherwise miss — that makes a big difference to the meaning of the sentence. How do you think Bittman and Sifton's dashes create a shout in their food reviews?

The dashes shout.

PARENTHESES

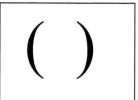

Parentheses whisper.

And you also always need two.

Parentheses whisper. They are the cornstarch of writing. In other words, like cornstarch, parentheses thicken a sentence by adding a little something extra even though it's completely non-essential. That's the rule for using parentheses: they enclose side commentary that whispers additional but non-essential information. They create intimacy (like you're sharing secrets) between reader and writer. Parentheses *whisper*.

For each sentence below, decide whether the italicized phrase should be a shout or a whisper.

1. I would much rather stay home and work on my writing *I'm tired of parties* so I can experiment with flair.

2. The last time I cooked anything *other than macaroni and cheese* I almost burned down the house.

3. I could eat an entire cheesecake *although I won't* right now.

4. Parentheses addict us *worse than chocolate* because once we start using them, we often cannot stop.

5. I used the verb "chronicled" yesterday since I've exhausted my other new verb choices *grappled, highlighted, expunged* .

6. I subdued my grill last night *I've worked all semester to tame that thing* and made the best hamburgers in Pennsylvania.

7. It snowed 2 feet *that's 24 inches* last night.

8. It snowed 2 feet last night *which means I skipped class.*

9. My ideal career wavers between a priest and a doctor *they are, in fact, closely related* because I want to heal people.

10. I want to employ the dash *right at this moment* to add instant complexity to my writing.

Answer Key (also depends upon personal preference here):

1. Shout	4. Whisper	7. Shout	10. Shout
2. Whisper	5. Whisper	8. Whisper	
3. Shout	6. Shout	9. Shout	

COLON

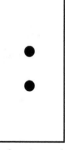

The colon introduces a definition or a list. It's like the waiter in a restaurant who explains the chef's specials or highlights the wine list. The colon reminds me of three things: a waiter, a tour guide, a teacher — all occupations that pause and explain — and adds a visual teaching moment into your paragraph.

A colon introduces a definition or list.

So Bittman writes,

> "The process requires separate cooking **processes: ginger** and garlic are crisped, leeks softened, rice and eggs fried."

He strategically uses a colon instead of a semicolon. The explanation of the cooking techniques follows the word "processes."

Or Sifton writes,

> "Baccalà was served three **ways: as** carpaccio, whipped, and baked."

He uses the colon because he *starts a list*. Easy as pie (or baccalà). Hint: a colon never follows a verb. Think of a colon as *replacing* the verb.

You try:

Write one sentence for a colon to introduce a definition.

Write one sentence for a colon to introduce a list.

COMMA

The comma salts writing. It joins the flavors of a sentence together, enhancing some parts and diminishing others. Sometimes you hardly notice it, but if it's used in the wrong way, or in the wrong amounts, everybody notices. A bad comma, like too much salt, ruins a recipe. Commas enhance the reading experience by allowing readers to follow along, to understand your meaning, and to properly digest it. Without commas, phrases run together like a runny egg overtaking the bacon and toast or turkey gravy assaulting your pumpkin pie. Not good.

Keeping phrases in their place means you reinforce good pace and rhythm (we'll talk about that in the next lesson), and you help the reader along. Without delving into the elaborate, historical rules of the comma, let's just get the basics down. You know how to use the salt without understanding salt's chemical names or history. I just want to hand you the salt shaker (not give you a lesson in chemistry).

Let's say you have a base sentence like this:

I went to the football game.

You can do all sorts of things to a sentence like this, but you need a comma to do it. Think of the comma as a little key that gives you permission to add some things onto a base sentence. If you want to add information to the beginning of the sentence, you need a comma.

Like this:

- After I tailgated, I went to the game. (You added on an introduction to tell us when, why, how, where, or who.)

Try some more:

- Even though I had bronchitis, I went to the game.
- Because I finished my paper, I went to the game.

Now, you need that little key if you want to add on to the **beginning** of the base sentence (like your ticket to the game), but if you tack it on to the **end**, you don't need it.

- I went to the game after I tailgated.
- I went to the game even though I had bronchitis.
- I went to the game because I finished my paper.

Words like these below are special types of conjunctions (subordinating) that don't need a comma when you add them to the end of your base sentence. They mix right into the base sentence like cream into your sauce. It's a smooth transfer with no need for a comma.

After	Once
Although	Only if
As	Since
As soon as	Though
Because	Unless
Before	Until
By the time	When
Even if	Whenever
Even though	Whereas
Every time	Whether or not
If	While
In case	
Now that	

But if you want to add on to the BEGINNING of the base sentence, you do need that comma. It's the permission to enter. It's like needing the invitation at the beginning of a party but not at the end when everybody's leaving.

- After I tailgated, I went to the party. (need the key)

- I went to the party after I tailgated. (don't need the key)

- I couldn't attend the event even though I planned on going. (at the end, so I don't need the key)

- Even though I planned on going, I couldn't attend the party. (beginning, so I do need the key)

But what about getting access to a party in the middle?

Easy, you still need comma permission.

- I went, after I tailgated, to the party.

- I went, even though I had bronchitis, to the party.

- I went, because I finished my paper, to the party.

REMEMBER: You have the base sentence. If you want to add some other ingredients, you need permission (a key).

Practice:
Here is your base sentence.

I wrote my paper.

1. Use an introduction to tell when, why, how, where, who, etc. Put the comma after the introduction.

   _____

   _____

2. Put the explanation of when, why, how, where, who, etc. at the end of the sentence. Don't use a comma. You don't need permission at the end.

   _____

   _____

3. Now put the explanation phrase in the middle of the base sentence. Put commas on either side of the phrase.

   _____

   _____

   - After going shopping with my mother, I wrote my paper.

   - I wrote my paper whenever I had my turn at the computer.

   - I wrote, whether I wanted to or not, my paper.

But what about other types of conjunctions? What if I'm connecting two sentences with coordinating conjunctions?

and, but, for, or, nor, so, yet

(I like to sing these words to the tune of "Twinkle, Twinkle, Little Star.")

The answer? Sometimes you need the key, and sometimes you don't. What determines your choice is whether or not what follows the comma is a complete sentence (a full thought with a subject and a verb).

Base sentence: **I didn't go to the party.**

I didn't go to the party, and I'm glad I stayed home.
I didn't go to the party, but I wanted to.
I didn't go to the party, for I had a paper to write.
I didn't go to the party, or my mother would have killed me.
I didn't go to the party, nor did I want to.
I didn't go to the party, so I stayed home.
I didn't go to the party, yet I still texted everybody there.

Why do you need comma permission here? Because you bring a guest along. Each phrase that follows your "Twinkle, Twinkle" word (a conjunction) drags along a new sentence. If what follows your conjunction is a FULL SENTENCE, you need the key.

Hint: If you remove that conjunction, you can use a semicolon to connect those sentences if you like.

When can I drop the key? If what follows the twinkle words is NOT a complete sentence.

I didn't go to the party and stayed home.
I didn't go to the party but wanted to.
I didn't go to the party for writing my paper.
I didn't go to the party or disobey my mother.
I didn't go the party so stayed inside instead.
I didn't go the party yet texted everybody.

Let's see if we can figure out why Bittman uses commas when he does. First, I'll underline all the "base sentences" for you:

> Like all fried-rice dishes, <u>you must start this one with leftover rice</u>; fresh rice is simply too moist. (Jean-Georges specifies jasmine rice, but white from Chinese takeout works nearly as well, and is more convenient.) Unlike most, <u>his is cooked in rendered chicken fat</u>, which has incomparable flavor. With the chef's blessing, <u>I tested the recipe with peanut oil</u>, which is fine. Perhaps not surprisingly — this is a chef's recipe, after all — the process requires separate cooking processes: ginger and garlic are crisped, leeks softened, rice and eggs fried. <u>But no step takes more than a couple of minutes</u>, and the recipe is absolutely worth the effort.

Bittman has several strong base sentences. When he wants to add some additional information onto the base, he uses that little comma key. In the first sentence, he just wants to supply an introduction that tells you starting with leftover rice resembles most fried-rice dishes. Easy, get the comma permission. In the second base sentence, Bittman provides "unlike most" to add another bit of introductory comment. The third base sentence embeds some additional commentary right in the middle, so we need those commas on either side as permission. Finally, notice the use of that "Twinkle, Twinkle" word and the comma to combine the last two sentences.

Practice:
Should you add commas? Why?

1. I assembled my résumé and cover letter.
2. I enjoy writing with flair because my writing improves each day.
3. Although I'm nervous about commas it calms me down to think about the commas as a permission key.
4. My cover letter uses some flair but I still don't like how it sounds.
5. I plan to attend your party but will come late.
6. I want even though it will be difficult to define my career.
7. I insist on using the flavor verbs although I don't know the meaning of some.
8. I'm going to my next class and then I'm going to lunch.
9. I printed out my paper at the lab yet my printer in my room still works.
10. Commas might be the hardest part of writing but I understand better how to use them.

ANSWER KEY:

1. I assembled my résumé and cover letter. (No need. No sentence follows the conjunction.)
2. I enjoy writing with flair because my writing improves each day. (No need because phrase occurs at the end of the sentence.)
3. Although I'm nervous about commas, it calms me down to think about the commas as a permission key. (Phrase at the beginning, so key is needed.)
4. My cover letter uses some flair, but I still don't like how it sounds. (Yes, because a complete sentence follows the conjunction.)
5. I plan to attend your party but will come late. (No, because no sentence follows the conjunction.)
6. I want, even though it will be difficult, to define my career. (Yes, because phrase breaks up the base sentence.)
7. I insist on using the flavor verbs although I don't know the meaning of some. (No need. See number 2.)
8. I'm going to my next class, and then I'm going to lunch. (See number 4.)
9. I printed out my paper at the lab, yet my printer in my room still works. (See above.)
10. Commas might be the hardest part of writing, but I understand better how to use them. (Yes, see number 4.)

As a final note about commas, remember that the glorious little comma lets you create variation in your sentences. You can add flavor because you know how to embellish your writing with conjunctions.

Commas also create some sentence complexity, but you have to be careful to use them correctly. I've only given you a few rules about commas—the basics—although so many more exist.

1. I haven't mentioned **commas that set off introductory elements created by prepositional phrases**, for example. Prepositions tell us something about the objects in our sentences. They give us information about where something is. The rules for prepositions are the same for the subordinating conjunctions. If you are using a prepositional phrase at the beginning of the sentence, you need permission with that comma.

Common prepositions: above, across, after, against, about, along, among, around, at, before, behind, below, beneath, beside, between, beyond, by, despite, down, during, from, in, inside, into, like, near, off, on, outside, over, past, throughout, under, up, upon, with, within, without

- Without my friends, I felt lost. (beginning, so use the comma)
- I felt lost without my friends. (at the end, so no need)

2. **Commas also set apart parenthetical information** (stuff that you could take out of a sentence without changing the meaning of the sentence).

- My aunt, the one who went shopping with me, turns 40 tomorrow.

3. You also **use commas for items in a series** (and yes, please use one before the final item).

- I packed clothing, make-up, a sleeping bag, and my book.

This concludes Lesson Two. Now that you know how to choose the most vivid verb (Lesson One), practice using advanced grammatical structures. I often have my students write me one paragraph that uses the Big Five. It's a fun challenge to include the romance, the teacher, the shout, the whisper, and the key in a single paragraph.

Often, when I compose blog entries, I attempt to add the visual flair of parentheses and dashes in particular. It's a way to modulate my written voice. It's a way to engage a reader in a conversation that now has a tone and a mood.

You can do it (it's not so hard after all). Write a sentence—just one—and see if you can embed dashes or parentheses at key moments. Then, show off your skills by using a semicolon; this punctuation mark creates instant complexity and credibility. Finally, think about having a teaching moment in your text with the double work of the colon: define a term or start a list. There. We did it, and it wasn't so hard.

Now, Lesson Three will teach you the art of condensing sentences and using variation to create rhythm. Get ready to simmer, stir, and taste your paragraph.

Lesson Three: Simmer, Stir, and Taste

Lesson Three:
Simmer, Stir, and Taste

Our stewpot brims with flavorful verbs and all the right secret ingredients. Now, we need to do three things:

1. We let things simmer and allow any excessive juice to reduce or condense.

2. We stir the pot and make sure everything blends well.

3. We taste our creation and adjust our spices to make things *just right.*

- **Lesson One** challenged us to find strong verbs.

- **Lesson Two** explained how to use some advanced grammatical structures to create complexity and credibility.

- **Lesson Three** will teach us how to eliminate unnecessary words (reduce) and then arrange sentences to create voice and rhythm (our unique taste).

We simmer things when we want to let the flavors blend and the juices reduce down. Reduction, as a cooking term, is *the process of thickening or intensifying the flavor of a liquid mixture such as a soup, sauce, wine, or juice by evaporation.* Reduction, as a writing term, is the process of intensifying the impact of your writing by eliminating unnecessary words and tightening (or thickening) the sentence construction.

One way to eliminate waste (unnecessary words) we know from Lesson One:

Tighten the verb form.

Now, we'll learn to tighten <u>the space</u> between the person and the verb. You want them snuggling up like warm butter melting over a biscuit.

<u>Sample Sentence:</u>

- The recipe that I wanted to cook was made by my mother in her kitchen after we had a discussion about how much I was missing her cookies.

We definitely need some simmering and reduction.

Step One: Find the person doing something. Underline that.

- The recipe that <u>I</u> wanted was made by my <u>mother</u> in her kitchen after <u>we</u> had a discussion about how much <u>I</u> was missing her cookies.

Step Two: Find the verbs.

- The recipe that I **<u>wanted to cook was made</u>** by my mother in her kitchen after we **<u>had a discussion</u>** about how much **<u>I was missing</u>** her cookies.

Step Three: Now reduce it!

Reduce the space between the person and the verb he or she performs. Also cut out any obvious or repeated concepts (redundancy). It's redundant, for example, to say that the mother cooks in the kitchen; she's obviously not cooking in the bathroom, right?

- My **mother made** my favorite cookies because **I missed** them.

See how the person and the verb sit next to each other?

26 words reduced down to 10.

Think about cutting your wordy sentences *in half* like this:

- The paper I have to write for English class was assigned by my professor to be due in 2 weeks. (20 words)

- My English **professor assigned** a paper due in 2 weeks. (10 words)

Try cutting your sentences down to ten words (as an exercise in reduction), and see how concise—how delicious—they become.

Lesson Three, besides REDUCING to intensify flavor, also teaches us to MIX our sentence patterns to create the best voice. In cooking, we talk about taste. **In writing, we talk about voice.** Writing should sound just as good as my mother-in-law's Christmas Caramel Cake tastes. When you mix up your sentence patterns, you create rhythm. When you create rhythm, you're making a voice come out in the writing.

By using the BIG 5 secret ingredients (semicolon, dash, parentheses, colon, comma), you make your writing have a unique rhythm. *But what about sentence length?* When you cook a stew, if it tastes too bland, you add some salt. If it's too spicy, you stir in some brown sugar to cut the spice. If it's too thick, you add some broth. If it's too thin, you add some flour or cornstarch as thickener.

In writing:

If it sounds too choppy, combine some sentences to elongate the beat.

If it sounds droning, add in some short (3-5 word) sentences.

If it sounds repetitive, change the sentence openings to create variation.

If it sounds anti-climactic, start with longer sentences, and add tempo by using increasingly shorter sentences.

If it sounds elementary, add in some sophisticated verbs, a semi-colon, and dashes. Use vocabulary that makes you sound more, er, *erudite.*

If it sounds too snobby, add in some slang, some short sentences, and some parentheses that make the audience feel part of the conversation. Admit some weakness somewhere.

CHOPPY

a lesson in pulling taffy

Let's take a look at a sample paragraph about writing:

- The best part of writing involves revision. I like to read my work out loud. I listen to the sentences. I see if they use the same pattern. I sometimes start every sentence the same. I put the main person doing something first. I need to start my sentences with different openings.

This paragraph has a drum beat to it that makes it choppy. In other words, the terse sentences torture the reader with a quick, almost frantic pattern. *The length of the sentences creates this problem*; each sentence has between five and eight words. That's like offering a guest a plate with just teaspoons of various desserts one after another. It's not enough, and it just leaves the reader feeling rushed and unsatisfied.

Try combining sentences (using commas if you need to), and don't forget that you might elongate sentences with the secret ingredient of a semicolon or colon. **Imagine that you are pulling taffy: elongate at least one sentence in a paragraph.**

Revision:
- The best part of writing involves revision. I like to read my work out loud **and** listen closely to the sentences **to see** if they use the same pattern. I sometimes start every sentence the same; I put the main person doing something first. I need to start my sentences with different openings.

You simply inserted a twenty-four word sentence to change a choppy pattern to a more elongated one; you added a full serving of cheesecake instead of that teaspoon of crust.

DRONING

a lesson in portion control

Consider that the paragraph has been elongated, but you elongated *too much*. You filled the plate with more than a mouthful.

- The best part of writing involves revision, and I like to read my work out loud and listen to the sentences to see if they use the same pattern. I sometimes start every sentence the same because I put the main person doing something first and need to start my sentences with different openings.

A simple revision: ***Add in a three-word sentence***. The short sentence acts like the bite of cranberry sauce to break up the mouthfuls of turkey and gravy.

- The best part of writing involves revision, and I like to read my work out loud and listen to the sentences to see if they use the same pattern. **It's worth it.** I sometimes start every sentence the same because I put the main person doing something first and need to start my sentences with different openings.

Great writers know the secret of the 3-5 word sentence to create voice. It works every time. In academic writing, when we want to analyze a text or report our research results, we tend to make the mistake of thinking that using long sentences means we sound *smart*. The more convoluted and lengthy, the more sophisticated we feel. The problem, however, is that we lose our audience. Put in a breather for them. Add a break. They'll love you for it.

REPETITIVE

a lesson in stirring

Finally, after elongating (but not too much), you want to stir up the pot by varying the structure of the sentences. Add some **introductory information** (like the when, where, how, why, who), and then add some **transitional phrases** to alert the reader of the relationship between sentences. Such phrases might include these words: because, likewise, however, finally, for example, in fact, etc.

- The best part of writing involves revision. **Before** I turn in a paper, I read my work out loud and listen closely to the sentences to see if they use the same pattern. It's worth it. **For example**, I sometimes start every sentence the same. **Because** I put the main person doing something first, I need to start my sentences with different openings.

You can even revise to add in the advanced grammatical structures:

- Writing — at least the best part — involves revision. Before I turn in a paper, I read my work (out loud) and listen closely to the sentences to see if they use the same pattern. It's worth it. For example, I sometimes start every sentence the same; because I put the main person doing something first, I need to start my sentences with different openings.

Notice the dashes that shout, the parentheses that whisper, the semicolon that connects, and the commas after introductory clauses. This writing uses visual flair and has the kind of complexity we want.

ANTI-CLIMACTIC

a lesson in anticipation

Say, for example, you want to create some drama for your reader. You want them to anticipate that something awaits them (like the smell of coffee and dessert from the kitchen while you eat your lasagna). Try starting with elongated sentences and then working toward shorter sentences.

Before:

- The best part of writing involves revision. Before I turn in a paper, I read my work out loud and listen closely to the sentences to see if they use the same pattern. It's worth it. For example, I sometimes start every sentence the same. Because I put the main person doing something first, I need to start my sentences with different openings.

After:

- The best part of writing involves revision. Before I turn in a paper, I read my work out loud and listen closely to the sentences to see if they use the same pattern. It's worth it. For example, I sometimes start every sentence the same. Because I put the main person doing something first, I need to start my sentences with different openings. Perhaps I might try a transitional phrase. I might try a different introductory phrase. It will take time. But I'll make a masterpiece in the end.

ELEMENTARY

a lesson in diction

What if your audience includes scholars attending an international conference on the process of revision? They've asked you to narrate your experiences. You want to sound smart. Easy, just put in some elevated diction. It's the same thing I do when I find out my coffee-connoisseur neighbor is coming for dinner. I bring out the expensive Indonesian Kopi Luwak blend.

Try this:

- The **most satisfying** part of writing involves revision. **Prior to** turning in a paper, I read my work out loud and **examine the sentence pattern.** It's worth it. For example, I sometimes start every sentence the same. Because I put the main person doing something first, I need to start my sentences with different openings. Perhaps I might **employ** a transitional phrase. I might **experiment** with a different introductory phrase. It will take time. But I'll **produce** a masterpiece in the end.

SNOBBY

a lesson in jargon

However, you want to be yourself. Pretending to sound smart by using ridiculous phrasing might make you look worse.

- As I commence my revision process, I vocalize my sentences to extricate the sentence constitution. What an advantageous enterprise this proves to be!

Let's try it all at once now.

Say, for a moment, you construct an argument about making better food choices (we are, after all, talking about cooking). You champion moderation in eating and drinking, and you favor choosing unprocessed food. Here's your first draft:

- "It's not important whether food is organic or local. It's not important if animals are raised humanely. These issues matter, but the paramount issue is to eat well. We must eat moderately. We must also limit our eating to real food. We must also consider that organic junk food is still junk food. There is plenty of organic junk food around. We can make these transformations. They require small changes. They will have a big impact. We can eat locally, eat organic food, and treat animals better because it will be only natural for all of this to happen."

Let's do a taste test:

Choppy?	Definitely. I feel like I have the hiccups in the middle of the paragraph. The sentences don't vary enough.
Droning?	It's more choppy than droning.
Anti-climactic?	Yes. I didn't feel the power at the end.
Elementary?	It could be more sophisticated.
Too snobby?	Some words seem too forced (like *paramount* and *transformations*).

Well, let's give this a little stir and add in some new spice combinations and secret ingredients. How would you do it?

Based on the suggestions from the previous page, we might:

1. Combine some sentences.
2. Add in an occasional short sentence.
3. Create some power at the end by including increasingly short sentences.
4. Add in some sophisticated diction (but not so much that it sounds condescending).
5. Add in some common expressions to make the writing seem warmer. Maybe include parentheses.

Here's the actual published paragraph, appearing in Mark Bittman's new book, *Food Matters: A Guide to Conscious Eating with More Than 75 Recipes.*

- "For the moment, let's ignore whether food is organic or local or even whether animals are raised humanely. All these issues matter, but the bottom line is that to eat well, we must eat moderately and limit our eating to real food. (Organic junk food—and there is plenty of it—is still junk food.) Once we make these strides, which require small individual changes but whose collective impact is huge, we'll be able to eat more locally, we'll be able to eat more organic food, and we'll be able to treat animals more humanely. In fact, this will come naturally."

What do you think of the changes? I think this paragraph tastes great. The writing has a better voice. Mark Bittman sounds like a nice guy, an educated guy, and a guy who really cares about all of us eating well. He does rely on some weaker verb forms, but by the end of the paragraph, he's using enough vivid verbs to keep us engaged.

Bittman's sentence pattern goes like this:

- introductory clause with comma
- base sentence with a comma and conjunction
- parentheses
- two introductory clauses with a base sentence that adds on a conjunction
- short base sentence

No two sentences follow the same pattern.
Now that's writing with flair!

One more thing. . .

As you consider the rhythm of your sentences and your diction, don't forget to think about *inflection*. Inflection in speaking refers to how we emphasize certain words. When you want to whisper in writing, you can use parentheses, but what if you want to emphasize but not shout with the dashes? What if you want to single out a particular word — one that you would say louder if you were speaking — without putting it in all CAPS or **ridiculously bolding and then underlining**? You don't want readers to FEEL LIKE YOU'RE SCREAMING AT THEM!

Instead of CAPS, underlining, or **bolding text** — which can be distracting — try the gentle, yet *powerful*, italics. Every once in a while (like maybe once or twice on a page), try to italicize a word that you want to pop off the page.

Let's *italicize:*

1. As an educator, I don't want students to memorize concepts. I want them to *learn*.

2. Finding professional journals in my field proves a difficult endeavor. Many nursing journals focus on communication, but they do not mention *therapeutic* communication.

3. The field of architecture seeks to harmonize man-made structures with the natural world. I devote myself to protecting the environment in urban settings. Your company's mission (unlike so many firms), *strengthens* the relationship between building and forest.

Try it:

When you read your writing aloud, words that need emphasis with your spoken voice might benefit from *visual* emphasis with italics. That's the final way to simmer, stir, and taste.

This concludes Lesson Three. Now that you know how to reduce your sentences, stir the pot with varied lengths and openings, and change the taste (tone) with various techniques, you're on your way to great writing. Lesson Four will add one more layer to your writing: garnish!

Lesson Four:
Garnish

Lesson Four: Garnish

Garnish : to enhance by adding decorative touches

You've done it. The last word sleeps peacefully at the end of your essay. Another essay well-written, another assignment sure to delight. You save the document and then curl up in your warm bed. But a thought haunts your dreams: What else might you have added? You survey your mind's store of flair—verbs, secret ingredients, voice—and wonder what touch you dare add to change your good writing to spectacular writing. You need one more bit of flair. But what?

Before Iron Chefs plate their creations on *Iron Chef America*, they always garnish the dish with some sprig of rosemary, some shaving of dark chocolate, some sliver of fresh lime. They arrange elements to highlight and embellish their creations.

In the world of writing, garnish represents wordplay or the art of being clever. Jay Heinrichs calls these rhetorical moves "instant cleverness" in his book, *Thank You for Arguing* (a great resource for even more garnish ideas). Cleverness endears the writer to the reader for two reasons: first, cleverness reveals the writer's quick wit and skill, but second, it acknowledges the *reader's* quick wit and skill in recognizing the moment of cleverness. Both parties feel good in the end. But savvy writing, like the elaborate garnishes you see in first-rate restaurants (the roses made of radishes, the apple carved into a swan in flight, the lemon constellations) take time, are often hard to construct, and sometimes don't come off as well as you imagine they will. Like expert food artists who work with tiny knives, our attempt at cleverness might seem awkward at first. Once we get the hang of it, though, the result stuns and rewards.

Garnish in writing assumes 10 main forms (although many more exist): puns, chiasmus, amplification, figures of speech, repeated first words, understatement, self-answering questions, editing yourself, making a noun into a verb, and allusions or imitation.

PUNS

I've heard it said that punning is the highest form of humor because it takes the most skill and thought. My husband is the master of the horrible pun, like when I wanted to park illegally with my hazard lights on, and he said, "Sweetheart, don't hazard that." Or when I'm asking how much pasta to make, and he says something like, "I don't know. Use your noodle."

Writers who pun know how to find the *double meaning* behind their wording. Puns make people laugh, roll their eyes, or furrow their eyebrows in confusion, but at least puns always awaken the audience. Puns make us feel part of the joke; we get it and can laugh along with everybody else. But puns can have another effect: they can make us stop and consider the weight of the words. The *Bible* contains the cleverest puns, most famously when proper names in the Hebrew dialect also have a meaning in the common language. Shakespeare, I've heard, uses over 6000 puns in his works, intended to prove political points as well as bawdy ones.

I've had students write great papers that embedded some clever puns like:

- Let me give you the skinny on childhood obesity.

  (*skinny* means information as well as referring to weight)

- Let's take charge of our credit card spending.

  (take *charge* means to control as well as purchase with a credit card)

- Supporting the childhood asthma fund just might take your breath away.

  (*breath away* relates to the problem of asthma and being astonished or impressed)

- Put down those cigarettes. Stop kissing their butts.

  (*butt* refers to a cigarette butt and also the idea of insincere behavior to get something)

- This paper explores the drama facing the Musical Theater major.

  (*drama* is a controversy and a theatrical play)

Try a pun in your assignments, and see how it feels. Just pick a word in one of your sentences that draws attention to itself because of a double meaning that plays with another word or concept in the sentence.

CHIASMUS

Chiasmus is a phrase where the second half inverts the first:

Ask not what your country can do for you

ask what you can do for your country.

~John F. Kennedy in his Inaugural
Address, January 20, 1961

("you" and "country" switch places in the second phrase)

Others:

- Years from now, how will we look back on today? As the **Great Recession**, or the **recession** that made us **great**? ~*Allstate Insurance television commercial*

- It's not a matter of whether we are **cheating** the **government** but whether the **government** is **cheating** us. ~*Jay Heinrichs' example in* <u>Thank You For Arguing</u> *regarding taxes*

- The purpose of this newspaper is to **comfort** the **afflicted** and **afflict** the **comfortable.** ~*Journalist Finley Dunne*

- **America did not invent human rights.** In a very real sense, it is the other way round. **Human rights invented America.** ~*Jimmy Carter in his presidential farewell address, January 14, 1981*

- What counts is not necessarily the size of the **dog** in the **fight.** It's the size of the **fight** in the **dog.** ~*Dwight D. Eisenhower, speech to the Republican National Committee, January 31, 1958*

- Never let a **fool kiss** you or a **kiss fool** you. ~ *Joey Adams*

- Let us never **negotiate** out of **fear**. But let us never **fear** to **negotiate**. ~*John F. Kennedy's Inaugural Address, January 20, 1961*

- **Mankind** must put an end to **war** or **war** will put an end to **mankind**. ~*John F. Kennedy in a speech to the UN General Assembly, September 25, 1961*

Notice that we frequently quote John F. Kennedy. Anyone wonder why? It's because he's so quotable! The chiasmus ensures we remember the words.

AMPLIFICATION

Amplification shapes a high-energy drama for your reader. It's easy: just make the last word or phrase of one sentence the first word or phrase of your next sentence. Amplification conjures a progression of events designed to create anticipation and energy. Although most useful for policy or rebuttal papers (or any project that requires an audience's understanding of cause/effect), you might still use amplification anytime you want to make a clever causal chain.

Here's one from one of my students.

- It might be a simple text message. The simple text message takes his eyes off the road for one minute. In that one minute, a mother drives through the intersection with her newborn baby in the backseat. That backseat crushes under the weight of his car that sped through the red light.

FIGURES OF SPEECH

Figures of speech show the reader that you know how to use common expressions that make a strong point. During political debates, you might hear a candidate say the politician "changed horses midstream" (he changed his position) or that the opponent is "straddling the fence" (she won't take a position). In your writing, good garnish might be a well-placed figure of speech. Bittman's expression in his book introduction, "takes these strides," is a figure of speech because he doesn't mean we literally take long steps with our legs.

Some figures of speech:

- Before we dive in. . .
- This makes a mountain of a molehill. . .
- This policy might just be a drop in the bucket. . .
- This author lets the cat out of bag in the first sentence. . .
- By the end of the proposal, the writer is way off base. . .

You probably use a dozen or so common expressions like these in your everyday speech. Try putting one or two in your paper. It relaxes the writing.

REPEATED FIRST WORDS

Repeated first words create instant rhythm and align your writing voice with the boom of the spoken word. You can't repeat first words and not think of Martin Luther King, Jr.'s repeated first words in his "I Have a Dream" speech.

You repeat the first word of your sentence to garnish a paragraph that wants to make an important point. Here are some examples from students:

- Now is the time to act. Now is the time to make a difference. Now is the time to cast your vote.

- Writing about blood creates pathos. Blood creates the emotional response. Blood makes us cringe in disgust. Blood makes us turn away.

- I cherish times with my husband. I cherish times with my children. I cherish times with my neighbors. Being a surgeon limits the time I have to connect with family and community.

UNDERSTATEMENT

Understatement embellishes writing by providing a sarcastic moment for readers to nod their head to. It's a way of making a point without shoving it in the reader's face.

- "It's just a flesh wound." (Black Knight, after having both of his arms cut off, in *Monty Python and the Holy Grail*)

- "A soiled baby, with a neglected nose, cannot be conscientiously regarded as a thing of beauty." (Mark Twain)

- "I have to have this operation. It isn't very serious. I have this tiny little tumor on the brain." (Holden Caulfield in *The Catcher In The Rye*, by J. D. Salinger)

Sometimes I hear these kinds of statements:

- The democrats haven't exactly solved the unemployment problem.

- *Fox News* sometimes exaggerates the truth a wee bit.

- My professor only assigned a mere 300 pages of reading by tomorrow. No problem.

You try: When you want to make a strong point, try doing just the opposite. Understate it for effect. But too much sarcasm alienates the reader. Just a few sprinkles here and there could drive your point home.

SELF-ANSWERING QUESTIONS

When you ask the reader a question, that's one way of engaging them (we'll talk more about that in Lesson 5). When you ask a question that you *answer* for the audience, it's a way of highlighting your point in the same way a nice mint leaf accentuates the basmati rice. Some students wrote:

- What's the worst thing that can happen? We lose the competition. What's so bad about losing? Nothing. We're used to it.

- The author creates a paradox through the male protagonist. Why does she do this? She intends to complicate a traditional viewpoint.

- Why would you want to hire a chemist to run your day-care center? I'm a problem solver, and I'm not shocked or overwhelmed by the chaos of any molecule, large or small, running around the room.

IMITATION

Imitating a style of a famous speaker or writer is one form of allusion. When you repeat first words, people might think of Martin Luther King, Jr. When you write stream-of-consciousness like Holden Caulfield talks in *The Catcher in the Rye*, people might think of J.D. Salinger. Writing an outrageous, sarcastic proposal will call forth Jonathan Swift. Find some writers you like, and mimic their tones and sentence patterns.

ALLUSIONS

Referencing pop culture, classical literature, political figures, or historical events promotes credibility and engages the audience. Depending on your audience, making a reference to a Lady Gaga song will keep them reading, whereas a Supreme Court Case ruling reference may not. If your audience cares about Shakespeare, then refer to as many plays as you can. Use a line, a character's name, a setting — anything to garnish the paragraph — as a way to magnify your knowledge and play into your reader's interests.

Can you recognize the following allusions?

- The author's language acts as his Patronus Charm that shields him from a critic's attack on his actual argument.

- The writer constructs a Catch-22.

- To write or not to write: that is the question.

NOUNS INTO VERBS

Verbing a noun happens frequently these days. I've seen the following verbs recently, and I have to admit, it's cool:

- Don't **synapse** too quickly between those arguments.
- Let's **architect** a different model for this program.
- The author **greenlights** the course of action.
- The writer **peppers** his prose with semicolons.
- Please **friend** me on Facebook.

You try: Invent your own.

As you generate various types of garnish in your writing, you want to remain vivid in your verb forms (Lesson One), complex in your grammatical structures (Lesson Two), varied in your sentence lengths and openings (Lesson Three), and clever in your use of wordplay (Lesson Four). As you architect your unique written voice, also remember to avoid expressions that lose their meaning from overuse. In writing, we call this cliché.

A note about clichés

Chefs want to create original creations. They don't want to be accused of cooking cliché. They don't want a panel of taste-testers to say, "No thanks, I've tasted this before." A cliché in writing is an overused expression. When you add those finishing touches of garnish, check to see if you use expressions that we've all heard so much they've lost their taste.

Imagine you read your cover letter or résumé, for example, and you use the following overused expressions:

- I take initiative.
- I want to make a difference.
- I think outside the box.
- I am motivated.
- I am a strong communicator.
- I am a team player.
- I want to be a success.
- I have exceptional organizational skills.
- I manage my time well.
- I have great interpersonal skills.

What's the solution to cliché?

USE AN IMAGE. Better yet, use an image and pepper in as many of the five senses (sight, sound, taste, smell, feel) as you can to engage your future employer.

I take initiative.
- This year, I realized the neighborhood children played video games more than hide-n-seek. I organized the Front Yard Fitness Campaign for 20 families to facilitate exercise and community building on my street.

I want to make a difference.
- Providing fresh water to Haitian children will save 600 lives a day. Having a small part of this project, to save even one of those children, justifies a lifetime of serving your company.

I think outside the box.
- When the Women's Shelter ran out of funds last year, I asked the local nursing home residents to knit 100 hat and mitten sets that I auctioned at my church for $50.00 each. We donated the money to the shelter and built two new bedrooms.

You try! Change the following popular clichés into image-driven sentences. For each phrase, imagine an example of each statement. Then narrate the story that goes with each example. Be concise!

- I am a strong communicator.
- I am a team player.
- I want to be a success.
- I have exceptional organizational skills.
- I manage my time well.
- I have great interpersonal skills.

This concludes Lesson Four. Now, you're ready to set the table and delight your guests!

Lesson Five:
Setting the Table

Lesson Five: Setting the Table

You're just about finished with *Flair*. You combine the flavor, the secret ingredients, the voice, and the garnish. You love your creation. But will anybody else? What if you serve up a luscious cheese fondue to lactose-intolerant guests? What if you ladle out the five alarm chili to an older crowd with heartburn and indigestion? Worse, what if you offend a group of staunch vegetarians with a platter of nearly raw lamb chops?

One can never divorce the act of writing from considering audience. The more you know your audience, the more likely you are to establish rapport.

If you imagine a dinner table, think of a collection of diverse people who hold differing political views. Think of different ages and attitudes. Think of different genders, histories, and socioeconomic backgrounds. Think of different geographies at the same table (a Texas rancher, a New York fireman, a Denver ski instructor, a Hollywood socialite). Think of different intelligences. Think of different tastes. Now try to imagine engaging all of these types differently.

Restaurants compile diverse menus for a reason. They want to please everybody by having something to offer for varying tastes. In the same way, great writers know how to entice diverse audiences. When you "set the table" in writing, you want to imagine these audiences and figure out ways to delight those seated. Maybe you write to a cynical student group. Maybe you write for political activists or for local organic farmers. Whoever they are, *knowing them well matters.*

The single most important factor in the effectiveness of your writing is the concept of rapport. Rapport is the relationship between two people; good rapport signals mutual understanding, trust, and a willingness to engage, while a lack of rapport indicates a writer's estrangement from his audience. **Therefore, it won't matter how much flair you use; the reader might not continue without feeling some attachment to the writer.** When a writer establishes rapport, he or she knits together a shared mental space that primes the reader to continue reading. But how can writers do this?

RAPPORT

Try some of the following techniques to "set the table" in a way that prompts even the most hostile reader to engage. These techniques don't just work in writing; they build connection when you're speaking as well.

1. **Dramatize what the reader might be feeling or imagining.**

   - "You might be wondering why such a topic matters in this economy."

   - "As you noted in your opinion piece, this election terrifies you."

   - "You must be thinking I'm just another rich kid from Philly."

2. **Invite the reader to consider what you are feeling or imagining.**

- "Like you, I'm bored with the topic of global warming. I'm tired of all the talking about the environment. I just want to see some positive change at the local level."

- "At first, considering Camus' argument alienated me. I didn't want to think about the futility of suffering."

3. **Pose a fantastic question that demonstrates genuine curiosity.**

When you ask an authentic question (one you truly care about and try to work out in the paper), then you prompt reader and writer to work together to arrive at truth.

- How can we know what success is?

- What difference does it make how we define "beauty"?

- Is the soul immortal?

- Why does the author compare the surgeon to a priest?

4. **Attach your essay to a larger conversation happening in the community, the nation, or the world.**

- "Our city reported hundreds of H1N1 cases last week alone. Residents worry over the availability of a timely vaccine."

- "Many people attended the Pro-Life rally in D.C. this month. The question for many activists is the issue of late-term abortions."

5. **Gain Buy-in and Promise Pay-off.**

Great writers know how to renew urgency about a topic; they create buy-in by showing what's at stake in not reading their words. They likewise promise pay-off by hinting at what the reader will gain in finishing the text. If a reader knows, in advance, what they will learn, how they might be changed, or how the topic will make a difference in the world, they'll most likely read on.

- "Tolstoy's text offers insight into how one manages failure and disappointment."

- "Thinking about recycling doesn't just change your campus. It changes the world."

- "A misunderstanding of the advertising career dooms future marketing professionals."

6. Acknowledge the audience and check for understanding.

When we speak to friends, we often stop and say things like, "Does this make sense?" or "Did you get that?" In writing, when you stop to acknowledge the audience and check for understanding, it's like when the tour guide pauses to make sure everybody has caught up with the group. You establish rapport because you prioritize your readers. Try these phrases:

- In other words. . .

- So far we've talked about. . .

- Another way of understanding this concept is. . .

- Some people might be confused at this point, but let me reiterate. . .

- If this doesn't make sense, let's look at it this way. . .

7. Vary your style to keep the attention of your readers.

Communication modes change with rapidly advancing technologies, and our attention spans normalize to keep pace with multiple messages that come to us immediately and in various forms (like right now, you might be texting, watching YouTube, Facebooking friends, reading these words, watching MTV, G-chatting, checking email on your iPad, typing an essay, and listening to your MP3 player). Speakers can use various technologies, but writers don't have as much available to them. We can, however, invent ways of changing writing modes.

In writing, easy ways to "vary style" might be to:

- Embed a picture, a text box, a bullet point list, or anything that visually breaks up the text.

- Insert a narrative using massive amounts of sensual detail.

- Employ the Lesson 3 suggestions to change the textual rhythm.

Besides these seven strategies, you can set the table by helping audience members understand your ideas by using *analogies*.

RAPPORT AND ANALOGIES

8. **Generate an analogy to help a reader connect to your point.**

Analogies require both parties to believe the same basic truths about the same basic things. If you can get someone to believe the first part of your analogy, they almost always track with you as you make your point with the second part of the analogy. Analogies advance your point, but they do it in ways that establish rapport. The analogy depends upon audience participation and therefore goes a long way in building a positive relationship.

- Bono, in his 2004 commencement address to the University of Pennsylvania, begins with this statement: "I don't think there's anything certainly more unseemly than the sight of a rock star in academic robes. **It's a bit like when people put their King Charles spaniels in little tartan sweats and hats.** It's not natural, and it doesn't make the dog any smarter."

  Bono establishes rapport by *making a self-deprecating analogy.* He wants to say that he feels uncomfortable, so he makes an analogy about dogs.

- **"Politicians are a lot like diapers**. They should be changed frequently and for the same reason." (*Man of the Year*)

- When Vince Vaughn accepted an award for *Wedding Crashers,* he said, "I feel a little guilty about winning the award because it's not that hard to do. When you work with someone like Owen Wilson, **I kind of feel like a jockey on the back of a great horse like Secretariat.** My job is just to hold on."

- Baz Lurhmann in his famous "Everybody's Free (to Wear Sunscreen)" speech: "Don't worry about the future, or worry, **but know that worrying is as effective as trying to solve an algebra equation by chewing bubblegum.**"

- Henry Kissinger, in a memo to President Richard Nixon on September 10, 1969: "**Withdrawal of US troops will become like salted peanuts to the American public;** the more US troops come home, the more will be demanded."

Here are some student analogies:

- Smoking cigarettes for the rest of your life is like running with the bulls; eventually, it will catch up to you and kill you.

- Race dialogue facilitators must address racism in tangible ways; simply acknowledging the elephant in the room is not enough to make it go away.

- Starbucks is like the crazy ex-girlfriend you still visit. You know you shouldn't, but you're drawn like a moth to the flame.

- Saying my family is not my real family because my mother did not give birth to me is like saying an apple isn't real unless you grow it yourself.

- Saying fraternity brothers are all selfish party animals is like saying all CEO's scam their coworkers like Bernie Madoff.

- Claiming the combination of genetic engineering and fertility science will lead to evil is like claiming all marriages will end in divorce.

- Believing I can learn how to be a psychologist by just "watching people" (without attending college) is like believing a student can just observe paintings in a museum to learn the art of painting.

Building an Analogy

Building an analogy for your readers takes some careful thought. You want to imagine what will most resonate with the person or crowd you address. For example, let's start building a simple analogy.

Imagine you want to apply to medical school, but your entrance exam (MCAT) scores are below average. You want to defend yourself and make the claim that a standardized test doesn't determine your future success as a doctor. You say this in your defense as a way of exposing a *false cause* logical fallacy:

Claiming the MCAT accurately predicts how well someone will do in medical school is like claiming. . .

FIRST: Identify the parts of the analogy.

MCAT	Medical School
A written exam	*Advanced study/ practice*

NOW: Build an analogy based on SIMILAR objects or ideas that your audience (in this case, medical school interviewers) cares about.

Surgery Textbook	Surgeon
Also a written document	*Also a specialized practice*

THEN: Put it all together.

Claiming the MCAT accurately predicts how well someone will do in medical school is like claiming. . .

> **that someone who memorizes a surgery textbook will be a great surgeon.**

Finally, offer a bit of explanation to drive the point home by adding, "Regurgitating facts on an exam doesn't take into account one's talent, skill, and passion." After one student used this analogy, a friend added on by saying, "Yeah, having a rope doesn't make you a cowboy."

Let's try another one:

In the 2008 movie, *Flash of Genius*, viewers watch Robert Kearns, the inventor of the intermittent windshield wiper, battle the Detroit automakers who steal his idea. In court, the auto company (with their high profile lawyer) claims Kearns didn't invent anything because *technically* all the parts he used for his invention already existed and could be purchased from any catalog.

Just when we think it's over for Kearns, the inventor (representing himself) makes a final plea to the jury. Rather than telling the jury, "This is a verbal fallacy of division," (meaning because the parts of invention aren't original then the whole cannot be original) **he uses an analogy** to win the hearts and minds of the audience.

Kearns holds up a book by Charles Dickens, *A Tale of Two Cities*, and reads the first couple of lines. They he asks the witness if he thinks Dickens *invented* any of the words in that book. The witness responds, "No." Then Kearns famously claims:

> *"I haven't checked, but I'm pretty sure there's not a single word in this book that is new, and they can all be found in a dictionary. All Dickens did was arrange them into a pattern. He created something new by using words, perhaps the only tools that were available to him just as almost all inventors have had to do in history."*

In other words, Kearns might have said:

"Arguing I didn't invent the intermittent windshield wiper because the parts already exist in a catalog is like arguing that Dickens didn't write *A Tale of Two Cities* because the words exist in a dictionary."

Now *that's* a flash of genius.

Let's see how to build this analogy:

Arguing I didn't invent the intermittent windshield wiper because the parts already exist in a catalog is like arguing that...

FIRST: Identify the parts of the analogy.

Windshield Wiper	Catalog
Original creation	*Written collection / list of something*

NOW: Build an analogy based on SIMILAR objects or ideas that your audience would understand.

A Tale of Two Cities	Dictionary
Also an original creation	*Also a written collection/ list of something*

THEN: Put it all together.

Arguing I didn't invent the intermittent windshield wiper because the parts already exist in a catalog is like arguing that...

> **Dickens didn't write** *A Tale of Two Cities* **because the words exist in a dictionary.**

Practice: When you want to expose someone's illogical reasoning, try building an analogy. Get friends and family to help!

A final note about RAPPORT:

Finally, think of you and your reader as being on a journey together. **Your writing invites the reader to join you on the journey.** Just like you wouldn't ignore your friend on the plane or refuse to talk to him at a restaurant, keep talking to the reader by explaining where you are going with your words. Imagine yourself as the cooking school chef who pauses every once in a while to make sure his students are following along.

9. **On the journey, use TRANSITIONS between paragraphs.**

Adding new information:	also, furthermore, additionally, likewise, moreover
Showing a consequence:	as a result, consequently, therefore, hence
Giving an example:	for example, for instance, as an illustration
Emphasizing a point:	above all, especially note
Comparing / Contrasting:	conversely, on the contrary, similarly
Reminding of order:	first, to begin, next, later, meanwhile
Concluding:	after all, in conclusion, to summarize
Restating a point:	in essence, in other words, namely

With rapport established with these nine techniques above, you might now ask whether or not your writing *actually persuades*. Some argue that all writing is an act of persuasion, so how does one persuade well? I like to think of rhetoric (language used to persuade) in terms of utensils you offer — or tools you use — to entice the reader to eat, or in this case, *read.*

Without forcing us to read the history of rhetoric or exhausting us by technical terms, let's just name three: ethos, pathos, logos. Or, for our purposes: the fork, spoon, and knife.

When you entice the audience to see things your way, you want to persuade them by your good character, credibility, and expertise (ethos). You also hope to arouse their emotions, eliciting sympathy, anger, surprise, compassion, or whatever emotion best suits your purpose (pathos). Finally, you want to engage the audience's good reasoning skills (logos).

How does one persuade well?

- Ethos: the character and credibility of the writer

- Pathos: the emotional appeal of language

- Logos: the logical reasoning within the text

Let's consider the various ways we might engage our readers by using these rhetorical appeals.

ETHOS:

Think of your ethos as your good name. And like the fork that makes it really easy for someone to eat, ethos guarantees your trustworthiness in the mind of the reader. Without it, readers have no reason to continue reading. They might say, "Who is this person? Why do I care what she has to say?"

To create ethos, writers have many options. Here are a few tried and true ways of establishing your good reputation and authority to discuss any issue.

- **Personal Narrative:** Mention personal connection with the topic through a narrative or a simple sentence that displays your experience.

- **Conversion Experience:** Write a "conversion experience" in which you show a change of mind. Conversion experiences often show the most credibility (which is why infomercials almost always feature the skeptic-turned-loyal fan). Begin the essay by claiming you used to believe one thing but then changed your position. That's powerful!

- **Use Insider Language:** Use language that reveals specialized knowledge of your topic. If you write about exorbitant tuition fees, use words like bursaries, franchised courses, and maintenance grants. If you write about the Go Green movement, use words like carbon footprint, bioaccumulation, GMO's (genetically modified organisms), or LOHAS (lifestyle of health and sustainability).

- **Ask a good question:** Use the techniques from the *Rapport* section to create your reputation as an inquisitive and thoughtful writer.

Ask yourself: What authorizes me to write this document?

PATHOS:

Pathos is the spoonful of sugar that makes the medicine go down. It's what makes the reader want to keep reading, even against their will. Why? Because you rope them in with the most powerful of rhetorical tools: emotion.

When you elicit an emotional response in your readers, you make them invest; they have an emotional tie that urges them to read on. How do we create pathos in our writing?

- **Sensory detail (smell being the strongest) about a situation in your text**: Writers hoping to generate funds for disaster relief know how to describe a scene with pathos; they might say that a hurricane or earthquake decimated a village, leaving smoky buildings, charred human flesh, and crying children behind. Likewise, a writer who wants to capture the importance of caring for our environment might paint a picture of a polluted world – toxic fumes, a treeless skyline, oily rivers – to encourage the reader to experience the situation.

- **Language with connotation (negative or positive) to produce a mood:** Choose words with a valence to sway the emotions. The verb quickly produces a mood. Consider the difference between saying, "The President *invited* students to *enjoy* his speech" and "The President *demanded* that students *endure* his speech."

- **A narrative with vivid language that involves us in a** *story:* CNN's Anderson Cooper's international fame grew out of his journalistic style. He didn't just report the news, he ***told the story*** about the families affected by it.

Ask yourself: What emotions do I want my reader to feel?

LOGOS:

Logos is the knife of rhetoric that cuts straight to the point to engage the reader's reasoning skills. Logos demands the intellectual response of the reader by either asking him to work through a claim, consider a thought-process, or confront historical or scientific facts. Ask yourself what type of reasoning you use in your writing. A logos-filled paragraph might include:

- **Statistics, charts, graphs, or figures**
  According to the National Endowment for the Arts website, the NEA has awarded 4 billion dollars to support the arts.

- **Quotations from expert sources**
  We might reconsider our view of high school 'nerds.' As Bill Gates remarks, "Be nice to nerds. Chances are you'll end up working for one."

- **Well-phrased questions that engage the mind**
  Is honesty always the best policy? What if you've been asked to keep a secret? What if you lie to protect someone?

- **Definitions**
  Mental health, as defined by some psychologists, is "being able to tell an integrated life narrative."

- **Analogies**
  Billy Graham explains in his 1962 address to the Harvard Law School: "Jesus once said that the gate to the kingdom is narrow. But we are narrow in mathematics. We are narrow in chemistry. If we weren't narrow in chemistry, they'd be blowing the place up. We have to be narrow. We are narrow when we are flying a plane. I'm glad that pilots aren't too broad-minded and just come in any way they want to. And why shouldn't we be narrow when it comes to spiritual dimensions and moral laws?"

A Checklist for Setting the Table

Ethos:

- Do I establish my credibility in some way in this paragraph?
- Do I reveal my personal experience with this topic?
- Do I use language that shows my connection to this topic?
- Do I sound like a nice person? Do I make myself trustworthy?
- Do I establish rapport with my audience?

Pathos:

- What emotions would someone experience when they read this?
- Does this emotion match my purpose in writing?
- How could I create more emotional appeal through verbs and vivid detail?
- What moments in my text might benefit from a narrative?
- What emotions do I feel about this topic? Does the reader know this?

Logos:

- Where do I try to engage the reader's reasoning skills?
- Do I ask a question in my text?
- Do I rely on expert opinion, statistics, or personal testimonies to develop my argument?
- Do I summarize an opposing viewpoint and then advance my claim?
- Do I make good use of an analogy to logically persuade my reader?

Handling Fighting at the Table

Dinnertime arguments are a cliché in the movies; somebody says something inappropriate, and somebody else gets offended. Usually, the girlfriend storms out, and the boyfriend follows her into the kitchen. Tears ensue. The dog gets to eat the turkey that fell under the table, etc., etc.

Cliché aside, this question remains for us: What's the best way to avoid an argument? As we wrap up *Flair*, it's only fitting to end with the best advice I learned in all my years as a national debater. Here's the last great cooking tip I can offer:

Put in some love.

I know it's cheesy. It's as cheesy as when a mother says the secret ingredient in her homemade lasagna is "love." It's the truth, though.

If you write from a position of love, you will most likely have a captive audience. If you write from a position of *kindness*, believing that what you have to say is good for someone else, they'll most likely believe it. Facts do not persuade. Facts argue.

Facts do not persuade. Facts argue.

The following five "love" ingredients succeed in writing, dating, working, and parenting. They aid family, friend, and work relationships. Whenever you have to confront a person whose ideas differ from your own, move through the five steps of rebuttal to — not argue — but *persuade*. To conclude our Setting the Table Lesson, consider the follow persuasion techniques:

- Listen

- Summarize the Other's Viewpoint

- Find Common Ground

- Expose Weaknesses in Their Argument *Gently*

- Advance Your Position

Listen:

Concentrate and focus. Figure out what the audience cares most about. What emotions do they feel about the topic? Why? What's at stake for them?

A tip:
Ask a good question, and then sit back and really listen.

As a pre-writing activity, think about mentally asking your audience:

- Would you tell me more about what you think?

- What is this like for you?

- How did you form this opinion?

Summarize:

When you listen well, you can repeat back to the person what they think and feel. You write things like:

- You feel that . . .

- It sounds as if you mean . . .

- I understand that you believe this . . .

- This topic makes you think . . .

- Your position is . . .

Find Common Ground:

When you can make an opponent feel as if the two of you are really more alike than different, it's easy to have a conversation. During presidential debates, notice how frequently candidates use the language below. Great debaters know how to persuade opponents by showing how *alike* they really are.

- You and I both agree that . . .

- We both support . . .

- Both sides believe that . . .

- I completely agree with you when you claim . . .

Expose Weaknesses in Their Argument Gently:

Maybe in high school you learned about logical fallacies. Maybe you learned how to attack an opponent by screaming, "Hasty generalization!" Maybe you learned how to humiliate others by making a list of how bad their reasoning skills were. You could look at them, point a finger, and say, "You use a slippery slope argument here, a false cause there, and a straw man here."

The problem with pointing out logical fallacies is that they intend to shame someone and *not* persuade them. Your telling me that my argument begs the question or poisons the well doesn't convince me to change my mind. It just makes me defensive.

To expose a weakness in somebody's (friend, sibling, spouse, boyfriend or girlfriend, boss, professor) argument, **use a clever analogy to *show* them the logical fallacy.**

Turn back to the analogy examples. Look at the different analogies students use to show a weak argument. If you want to talk to someone about their smoking problem or their belief that all fraternity brothers binge drink, then use an analogy, not some pompous rhetorical term designed to shame.

Use an analogy,
not some pompous rhetorical term. . .

Analogies are hard. They take time to formulate. Below, I've listed some common logical fallacies: false cause, hasty generalization, and false choice. How would you complete these analogies to expose a weakness in reasoning?

1. Saying guns cause violence is like saying . . .
   False Cause: _____

2. Claiming that college students are all binge drinkers is
   like saying . . .
   Hasty Generalization:_____

3. Saying I can either be a mother or have a career is like
   saying. . .
   False Choice:_____

Some Answers:

1. Saying guns cause violence is like saying the fork *causes*
   obesity.

2. Claiming that college students are all binge drinkers is
   like saying *all* writers are chain smokers.

3. Saying I can either be a mother or have a career is like
   saying I can *either* be a mother or a wife. I can be both at
   the same time.

Analogies work. Last night I saw an ad in a glossy, expensive
magazine. An advertisement was trying to explain why the
magazine industry won't be destroyed by the Internet. Just
because digital media exists doesn't guarantee that hard-copy
magazines won't exist anymore. Here's the analogy from the
"Magazines, the Power of Print" campaign:

Will the Internet kill magazines?

Did instant coffee kill coffee?

Advance Your Position:

When you try to change someone's mind to believe what you believe or do what you do, you want to advance your position in a way that acknowledges *them* in the whole process. Otherwise, you risk losing their attention before you even begin. When you write your argument, try the following:

PREDICT what they will object to:

- At this point, you might be thinking . . .
- This point likely angers you for this reason . . .
- Most of you worry about this point . . .

SOOTHE their concerns in advance:

- Let me assure you . . .
- Your concerns are valid, and I've been thinking about them as well.

and **DISPLAY HOW BENEFITS OUTWEIGH COSTS:**

- The advantages to this (plan, idea) mitigate any concern you have . . .

Remember:

When you showcase how your position benefits your audience—that their well-being matters to you—then that audience will want to listen. Persuasion focuses on the well-being of the listener, NOT the ability of the writer to win or argue.

**Persuasion focuses on the well-being
of the audience,
NOT the ability of the writer to win or argue.**

Finally. . .

Think about your audience. Imagine their lives, their jobs, and their interests. What do they know about your topic? How are they feeling? What concerns them the most? What is at stake for them in this writing? How can you then shape your writing to suit your audience?

What do you know about your audience? Think about:

Gender

Race

Religion

Education

Geography

Background

Cultural Trends

Insider Language

Marital Status

Occupation

Hobbies

The more you know about your audience (like your dinner guests), the more you can shape your writing (and set your table) with flair.

This concludes Lesson Five. *Take a deep breath.* If you feel overwhelmed, just remember five easy steps: find flavor with that verb; use a few secret ingredients; simmer, stir, and taste your paragraph; garnish your work, and set a beautiful table.

Conclusion

Conclusion

We stand again before the big stew pot in the kitchen. You know how to find flavor and use secret ingredients. You know how to add garnish and set a proper table. But right now, you wonder what in the world you're supposed to cook. In writing language, we call this stage *invention*. I tell my students that, for most writers, invention is the hardest stage of writing.

Invention is the hardest stage of writing.

Coming up with topics means you have to dig deep, take a risk, and find something to care about. It's like on *Iron Chef*. Someone gives you a bunch of ingredients, and you scurry around, wiping your hands on your shirt and sweating as the clock ticks. But eventually, you take a deep breath, remember what you know, and all of a sudden, *invent a masterpiece*. Before you begin a writing project, write down everything you know about the topic. Then, try asking the following questions:

1. What about this assignment **excites** me most?

2. What **angle** might I take to further this enthusiasm?

3. What **unique contribution** can I make to the conversation surrounding this topic?

So if a professor or a supervisor assigns you a writing task, find a way *in*. Find a way to care deeply about it. It's like when a chef presents you with escargot or frog legs or okra. You might think to yourself that you could never, under any circumstances, enjoy such a meal. But wait! You *might*. Take a sip of water, cleanse the palette, and prepare yourself for an adventure.

You can do it. Let something stir you. Claim this something as your own angle. Then dig in and offer your thoughts.

Excitement.   *Angle.*   *Contribution.*

We are all waiting to read what you have to write.

Finally, note the frequency of cooking show disasters. We shriek when the gorgeous cake topples onto the floor or when the stuffed duck slaloms off the platter and into the dishwater on live television (in high definition). We gasp and wonder what we might have done with such a failure. If we were Julia Child, we'd pick the duck back up, rinse it off, and carry on. We'd see the accident as an opportunity for embellishment; we'd add some garnish and smile. Or—if we were being honest—we'd go hide in the bathroom and cry. Maybe at our best moments, we would laugh at ourselves and start over.

Like in those cooking shows, writing disasters happen. And when they do—because they will—we can choose to be gentle with ourselves. Nobody ever makes a perfect cake the first time (even the Cake Boss). But if you take your time, go back to the basics, and *practice*, something great emerges from the oven.

Writing disasters happen.

You'll have hundreds of writing occasions in your lifetime. Such occasions for writing allow opportunities to use vivid verbs (Lesson One), experiment with advanced grammatical structures (Lesson Two), create an authentic voice (Lesson Three), display some pizzazz (Lesson Four), and finally demonstrate genuine concern for the well-being of the audience (Lesson Five). On the following page, I've included a *Flair Checklist* for your writing.

I hope you've enjoyed *How to Write with Flair.*

Flair Checklist

1. Do I use vivid verbs?
2. Are my verbs in their strongest form (cutting board test)?
3. Do I juggle some secret ingredients throughout my writing (semicolons, dashes, commas, parentheses, and colons)?
4. Do I "stir the pot" with varied sentence structures and lengths?
5. Have I embellished my writing with garnish in some form?
6. Have I analyzed my audience? Do I know them?
7. Do I attempt to build rapport with my readers?
8. Does my diction match my intent and my audience?
9. Have I shown my audience that I understand them and have listened to them?
10. Would my audience feel cared for by me? Do I put in some love?
11. Do I appeal to emotion in this writing (pathos)?
12. Do I seem trustworthy (ethos)?
13. Do I engage the reader's reasoning skills (logos)?
14. Do I make use of good transition sentences?
15. Have I demonstrated the importance of my topic? Do I tell my readers why this writing matters?
16. Was I able to form an analogy to advance my point?
17. Did I enjoy the process of writing this paper? What can I do differently to celebrate the writing task?
18. Do I offer a unique contribution to the conversation surrounding my topic?
19. Do I avoid cliché in my writing?
20. Is this writing memorable?

About the Author

Heather Holleman teaches composition classes at Penn State. Dr. Holleman earned the *Moscow Prize for Excellence in Teaching Composition* and *Rackham's Most Outstanding Graduate Student Instructor Award* while at the University of Michigan. She also served as a Sweetland Fellow in the University of Michigan Writing Center. At Penn State, Dr. Holleman directed the Excellence in Communication Certificate Program for the College of Liberal Arts while providing leadership and training for the Advanced Writing instructors.

Her favorite punctuation mark remains the semicolon. She attempts to use the verb "grapple" at least once a day.

She blogs daily at *Live with Flair.*

www.livewithflair.blogspot.com

CPSIA information can be obtained
at www.ICGtesting.com
Printed in the USA
LVHW022245130721
692597LV00010B/292